JERUSALEM

WALTER ZANGER

THE GREAT CITIES LIBRARY

A BLACKBIRCH PRESS BOOK

WOODBRIDGE, CONNECTICUT

Published by Blackbirch Press, Inc.
One Bradley Road, Suite 205
Woodbridge, CT 06525

©1991 Blackbirch Press, Inc.
First Edition

Printed in Hong Kong
Bound in the United States of America

Editors: Kailyard Associates
Maps: Robert Italiano
Photo Research: Photosearch, Inc.

Library of Congress Cataloging-in-Publication Data

Zanger, Walter.
  Jerusalem/Walter Zanger.
  (The Great cities library)
  Includes bibliographical references and index.
  Summary: Surveys the four thousand-year history of the Holy City and its
religious, political, and cultural importance to Jews, Christians, and Mos-
lems.
  ISBN 1-56711-022-3
  1. Jerusalem—History—Juvenile literature. 2. Jerusalem—History. I.
Title. II. Series: Great cities (New York, N.Y.)
  DS109.9.Z36   1991
  956.94'42—dc20   91-10829
                                                                  CIP
                                                                  AC

pages 4–5
A view of the Old City from the Tower of David.

CONTENTS

JERUSALEM

AMERICAN COLONY
Tomb of the Kings
Cathedral of St. George
W.F. Albright Institute of Archeological Research
WADI EL JOZ
BET YISR'AEL
Site of the Mandelbaum Gate
U.S. Consulate
ME'A SHE'ARIM
Romanian Church
Church of St. Stephen
Rockefeller Museum
Garden Tomb
Herod's Gate
Armenian Mosaic
MORASHA
Damascus Gate
Sheikh Lulu Mosque
MUSLIM QUARTER
Monastery of the Flagellation
Church of St. Anne
Ecce Homo Arch
St. Stephen's Gate
Tomb of Mary
Garden of Gethsemane
New Gate
El-Khanqa Mosque
CHRISTIAN QUARTER
Church of the Holy Sepulchre
Church of the Redeemer
Church of John the Baptist
Haram Esh Sharif
MT. MORIAH
Dome of the Rock
Golden Gate
Church of the Pater Noster
Church of Mary Magdalene
MOUNT OF OLIVES
Hebrew Union College
Jaffa Road
Jaffa Gate
Wailing Wall
Temple Mount
Tombs of the Prophets
Intercontinental Hotel
The Citadel (Herod's Palace)
ARMENIAN QUARTER
JEWISH QUARTER
Hurva and Ramban Synagogues
Al Aqsa Mosque
Islamic Museum
King David Hotel
Cathedral of St. James
Dung Gate
City of David Archeological Garden
Jericho Road
Tomb of Herod's Family
Armenian Art Museum
Sephardic Synagogue Complex
Church of the Dormition
Zion Gate
David's Tomb and the Room of the Last Supper
MT. OPHEL
KEFAR HA-SHILOAH
MT. OF OFFENCE
Montefiore Windmill
MISHKENOT SHA'ANANNIM
MT. ZION
Pool of Siloam
N
Bethlehem Road
0   1/4 miles
0   1/4 km.
JERUSALEM

LEBANON
SYRIA
Mediterranean Sea
ISRAEL
JERUSALEM
JORDAN
EGYPT
SAUDI ARABIA

6

The Lion of Judah

And I lifted my eyes and saw, and behold, a man with a measuring line in his hand! Then I said, "Where are you going?" And he said to me, "To measure Jerusalem, and to see what is its breadth and what is its length." (Zechariah 2:1-2)

Names: In Hebrew: Yerushalayim ("city of peace"); in English: Jerusalem; in Arabic: Irusalim al-Kuds ("the holy"). Ancient names: Shalem (Gen. 14:18), Jebus (Joshua 15:8, Judges 19:10).

Population: Inside the Old City walls: 26,000; total population: 460,000. Approximately 310,000 are Jews, approximately 145,000 are Muslim Arabs, approximately 15,000 are Christian Arabs.

Size: Part of the city is still enclosed by the Old City walls, built by the Turks in the sixteenth century. Area inside the Old City walls: 215 acres; total area: 26,000 acres.

Symbol: The Lion of Judah.

Commerce and Industry: Jerusalem, as capital of the State of Israel, is the site of the Knesset (the Israel Parliament) and most government ministries, which are the major employers in the city. Since Jerusalem is an important tourist and pilgrim destination (more than 1,400,000 tourists in 1989), many thousands of people are employed in tourism jobs. There is some industry in the city, but it is intentionally of the high-tech and non-polluting kind. Although the city is the country's capital, Israel's commercial, banking, and industrial centers are located elsewhere.

Municipal Government: Every resident of the city, whether citizen or non-citizen, may vote in municipal elections. Each voter has two ballots: one for the mayor and one for the city council. The mayor is elected directly and the city council are elected proportionally for a period of four years.

THE PLACE

"Ten measures of beauty came into the world. Jerusalem received nine measures, and the rest of the world one."
— **Hebrew Proverb**

Evening descends on Jerusalem, as seen from the walls of the Old City.

Jerusalem is a hilltop city, lying close to the edge of a mountain range in the center of the land of Israel. The country lies on the coast of the Mediterranean Sea. Immediately to the east of the city lies the Judean desert. The ridge that separates the city from the desert is called (from south to north) the Mount of Annointing, the Mount of Olives, Mount Scopus, and French Hill—all of them are names for different parts of the same mountain.

Mountains

The city's average elevation is 2,500 feet (760 meters) above sea level, and this fact affects the climate, the possibilities for agriculture, population density, and the transportation network. In effect, its location on the mountain at the edge of the desert insured that the city was never to grow very large.

Jerusalem suffers from several geographical disadvantages. The city does not lie on any main road, and there is no important river nearby. Nor, for the same reasons, has it any strategic value in the defense of the land around it. It has only one spring, the Gihon, as a source of water, so it could never support a large population. (Until modern times the city depended mostly on rain water). It has no minerals or raw materials. And the land around it is mountainous and difficult to farm, so it never had a surplus of food. History rather than geography made Jerusalem a great city.

The Church of All Nations, at the foot of the Mount of Olives

Valleys

An aerial view of the valleys around the city reveals a pattern resembling a lopsided pitchfork standing on its handle. Each of the lines is a valley, eroded into the mountains by rainfall running off the hills and down to the desert.

On the west and south is the steepest and most dramatic of the three valleys, the Canyon of the Sons of Hinnom. In Hebrew, the word for canyon is "gai," and this is the only place in the area (and one of only two or three places in all of Israel) to bear that title. The "gai-Hinnom" is a valley with walls that are nearly vertical. It is a frightening place at night. In

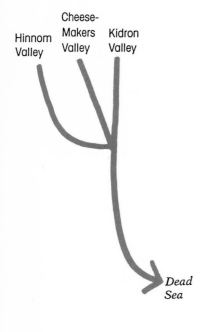

Hinnom Valley

Cheese-Makers Valley

Kidron Valley

Dead Sea

ancient times they used to burn garbage at the bottom of the canyon, and sometimes they even sacrificed children to the god Moloch at a place in the Hinnom called Tophet. The ancient Israelites remembered the Hinnom as a place of burning fires and scary rituals. So much so that "gai-Hinnom" became "Gehenna," a word for Hell, and one finds the word in Jewish literature, in the New Testament, and in the Koran.

Since the valley is so steep, it formed a natural southern and western border of Jerusalem for most of the city's history.

Hinnom, though most dramatic, is not the largest of the three valleys. The largest is called Kidron, and it is on the other side of town. It separates the city from the Mount of Olives to the east. Kidron drains much of the eastern Jerusalem mountain region and gathers up the rain waters that flow in the other valleys. It runs down to the Dead Sea, and it has always defined the eastern border of the city.

Between the two is a third valley, much smaller, called the Cheese-Makers valley. Very often one finds it referred to by its Greek name—"Tyropoeon" —though nobody knows how the valley got this strange name. For most of the city's history, the Tyropoeon ran right through the middle of town, as it does today. But there have been times, when Jerusalem was very small, that Tyropoeon formed the western border of the city.

The largest of the three valleys surrounding Jerusalem is Kidron, the site of the Tomb of Absalom.

Climate

The climate of Jerusalem is Mediterranean—long, dry summers and rainy, cool winters. During the summer, from about April through October, it does not rain. Since the city sits high in the mountains, it is rarely too hot and never too humid (average humidity: 62 percent). Heat waves come in the spring and fall, when the wind blows in from the Arabian desert. August is the hottest month, and the average temperature is 73° Fahrenheit (24° Celsius).

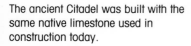

The ancient Citadel was built with the same native limestone used in construction today.

In the winter, from October through March, it rains in Jerusalem. The city has an average rainfall of about 25 inches, almost as much as England. The difference is that the rain only falls for about 50 to 55 days a year; therefore, the winter rains are harder than one might expect. The distribution of rain affects the growing seasons as much as the quantity of rain. In England, where it rains on an average of 300 days a year, but usually lightly, one finds green fields and flowers every month of the year. In Jerusalem, the land is green in winter and spring. But apart from parks and gardens, which must be irrigated, the land dries out for the whole summer, coming to life again after the first rains of the fall.

The city is about the same latitude as southern Georgia in the United States (31 degrees north latitude). But because of the mountains, it snows only every few years in Jerusalem. The temperature rarely goes below freezing, however, and the snow usually melts after half a day.

The Buildings of Jerusalem

The visitor in Jerusalem is always surprised at how easily and naturally the ancient city and the modern buildings mesh. People can sense, even if they can't express it, that some special thing unifies the whole city. The feeling is accurate; that something is stone—local Jerusalem limestone out of which every building in the city has been built, and, *by law,* must always be built, today and in the future. Jerusalem

The streets of the Old City are filled with vendors hawking their wares.

An archeological excavation near the
City of David

limestone is a comfortable and durable material. It
is smooth to the touch, a bit hard and edgy when you
first build with it, but softened, darkened, and im-
proved with age. The stone has a dozen different
shades: from a creamy white, through beige and a
rust-colored pink, to a light tan.

The effect of building an entire city out of this one
material is astonishing. Jerusalem is one of the few
cities in the world that is all one color! That color
changes as the limestone reflects the sunlight in
different ways at different seasons and different
times of the day. Because of the way light hits the
stone, the city has often been called "Jerusalem of
Gold." And in a full moon on a clear night, the city
seems to float in space.

The Walls

The wall around the Old City was built by the Turks in the mid-1500s. Until about 100 years ago, the entire city of Jerusalem was surrounded by a massive city wall and everyone lived inside it. But a city wall, no matter how imposing, is a structure like any other. Over the course of the centuries, as Jerusalem changed, the walls changed too. When prosperous, the city grew and its walls expanded to enclose new neighborhoods. When destruction and disaster overcame the city, the walls crumbled and the city shrunk.

Jerusalem was destroyed a dozen times over the centuries, resettled soon afterwards, and its walls were often rebuilt. Sometimes they were larger than before, but usually they were smaller as the city started anew. Thus it happened that the city walls of Jerusalem expanded and contracted like an accordion.

The city of Jerusalem today is in a condition nearly unprecedented in all its 4,000-year history. The overwhelming majority of its inhabitants live outside the Old City walls. This fact reflects the general sense of security that its inhabitants now feel about the place, and contrasts with what was the "normal" situation for thousands of years.

THE PAST

"The history of Jerusalem from the earliest times is the history of man, a history of war and peace, of greatness and misery, of splendor and squalor, of lofty wisdom and of blood flowing in the gutters."
—Teddy Kollek & Moshe Pearlman

Orthodox Jews pray at the Western (Wailing) Wall.

Jerusalem has a very long history. People have been living there and have been writing books about the city for 5,000 years. Ancient histories, stories, and poems are still read to this day. The books of Genesis, Samuel, Kings, Isaiah, Jeremiah, the Psalms, and the Gospels were written in Jerusalem. Jerusalem is where the Bible came from.

From Jerusalem came the most influential religions of the world: Judaism, Christianity, and Islam. Jews, Christians, and Muslims call Jerusalem the Holy City. And anyone who wishes to understand the Holy City of Jerusalem must be patient and let the old books and the old stones tell their story.

The Earliest Days

History begins when people start to write. For earlier periods before the invention of writing, one must depend on archaeological excavations. A great deal can be learned about a city and the way people lived by studying houses and walls, temples and fortresses, tools that were used, and the art that was created.

The earliest writing we have dates to around 2500 B.C., and the earliest written mention of Jerusalem came about 500 years after that. But we know from archaeology that the city was inhabited as early as about 3000 B.C.

A stone tablet shows an example of Arabic writing.

Its first inhabitants were a people the Bible calls Jebusites. They were an indigenous Semitic group, one of a number of peoples who shared the name "Canaanites." The Canaanites were the original inhabitants of the land of Canaan. They called the city Jebus, which is one of its oldest names.

Jerusalem of the Bible

King David of Israel captured the city and made it the capital of his kingdom in the year 1000 B.C. The town David captured and rebuilt, today is called the City of David. It was located on a low mountain spur south of the present walls of the Old City. The Kidron Valley was its eastern border and the Cheese-Makers Valley its border on the west. It may seem odd that the oldest part of town is now outside of town, but there was a reason for it being there. And there is a reason that it is no longer inside the walled city.

That reason can be spelled out in just one word: water. On the valley floor of the Kidron, below the City of David, is the only place around the city where there is a source of water—a small stream that still runs today called Gihon. Solomon was crowned king at the Gihon.

Until the invention of plaster (crushed, burnt lime-stone), in about 1000 B.C., every city in the world had

An ivory pomegranate believed to have come from the Temple of King Solomon, eighth century B.C.

Solomon's temple, as it was being built.

to be built right on top of a source of fresh water. After the invention of plaster, people could live anywhere. By storing rain water in cisterns—holes in the ground lined with plaster to hold water—people no longer needed to build cities on or next to water sources. Jerusalem after 1000 B.C., had enough water from cisterns and aqueducts that were filled by winter rains. It didn't need the spring any more, and the low spur of the city was too difficult to defend. So the city moved higher up the hill.

For a little more than 400 years, Jerusalem was the capital of a kingdom that included both Israel and Judah. During this time, the kingdom was threatened with military and political tensions. The threats came from Israel, which separated from Judah after the death of King Solomon, King David's son.

The other military threats came from the rise of the great kingdoms of early antiquity—Egypt, Assyria, and Babylonia. Egypt invaded Judah shortly after the death of Solomon and destroyed many smaller cities, but not Jerusalem. Assyria destroyed Israel, the northern kingdom, in 721 B.C. Twenty years later, the Assyrian king camped beneath the walls of Jerusalem, preparing its destruction. Only at the last moment was the siege lifted and the city spared.

Jerusalem's creativity derived from two factors. First was the unique position of Israel as the land bridge connecting the great empires of the world. Its location meant that traders and travelers had to pass through the land of Israel to go from Africa to Asia or Europe. This made the land a great trading center, and consequently very wealthy.

Solomon ruled at a time when all the great powers were in a period of decline. He knew how to exploit this situation. He established himself and his kingdom in the role of trader, broker, and merchant for the world.

The land bridge also exposed the people to a great mix of cultural influences unique to the ancient world. Israel, with Jerusalem as its capital, was the place where the Greeks, Egyptians, Mesopotamians, and the Jews met each other.

The second factor that contributed to the creative climate in Jerusalem was its importance to the Jews. David had brought the Ark of the Covenant—a portable shrine-throne that had accompanied the Jews throughout their wanderings, into the city. The Ark insured that Jerusalem would become the cultural and spiritual center of the Jewish people. David's son Solomon inherited the kingdom and brought it to unprecedented prosperity and influence. A network of roads developed from the capital city to the farthest ends of the kingdom. On them traveled the king's bureaucrats. To ensure Jerusalem's spiritual centrality as well, Solomon built the Temple of the Lord on the hilltop north of the city. The city as a spiritual center survived the breakup of the kingdom and was exposed to continual foreign influences.

King David brought the Ark of the Covenant to Jerusalem, which made the city the center of Judaism.

As the city became great, it struggled to retain the religious and spiritual vision that had inspired its founders. At every stage of its Biblical history Jerusalem had prophets walking the streets and palaces. They warned the kings and the people not to give up the ethical and moral standards required by the God who had led them there. Isaiah, Jeremiah, and Ezekiel were prophets of Jerusalem. They taught a revolutionary doctrine—that there was a God-given law to which even the king of the land was subject. Violation of the law, by king or commoner, was certain to bring punishment from God. Therefore, the doing of good and the avoidance of evil had political value. The prophets were very political figures in an age when no common man had ever dared address—let along threaten!—a king. The conflict between God and *mammon* (material wealth or possessions) was played out in Jerusalem. Much of the Bible comes from this period of the Judean kings.

The city grew as it prospered. It crossed the Cheese-Makers valley and may have reached the Hinnom valley to the west. Pieces of walls and houses have been found on the western hill, but scholars are still not certain of the city's exact dimensions.

Exile and Return

In the end, brute force won the day. In 586 B.C., the city was destroyed by Nebuchadnezzar, king of

Babylon (modern-day Iraq). The people of Jerusalem were sent into exile "by the waters of Babylon," that is Mesopotamia, between the Tigris and Euphrates rivers.

The Persians destroyed Babylonia in 539 B.C. Cyrus the Great, king of Persia, issued a decree allowing the Jews to return to Judah. Sheshbazzar, assumed by scholars to have been the son of one of the last kings of Judah, led a small group back from exile and began to rebuild Jerusalem. Zerubabel, a priest who accompanied Sheshbazzar, was credited later with supervising the reconstruction of the Temple, dedicated in the spring of 515 B.C.

This remains an obscure chapter in the history of Jerusalem. Ezra and Nehemiah, Jewish nobles, came to govern the province of Judah around 440 B.C. Nehemiah was the one who actually seems to have finished the construction of the city walls. Their Jerusalem was much smaller than the biblical city had been. But from this modest re-beginning, Jerusalem grew to be larger than it had ever been before, or would ever be again.

The Second Temple

Alexander the Great (356–323 B.C.) conquered Greece and most of the Middle East, including Egypt and part of Asia. A region that included Judah was renamed Judea under Greek, and eventually Roman, rule.

Alexander the Great conquered most of the known world some 300 years before the birth of Jesus.

After Alexander's death, Judea was ruled by one of his generals, Ptolemy. This was a relatively quiet period. But then, in 198 B.C., the Seleucids, people who were loyal to the general Seleucus, beat the Ptolemys in a fierce battle. Jerusalem, along with the rest of the region, was passed to Seleucid control.

Rebellion and Prosperity

The Seleucid king, Antiochus IV, did something nobody had ever done before. In the 160s B.C., he began a campaign of persecuting (punishing) the Jews in order to move attention away from the failures of his government. He defiled the Temple and tried to force the Jews to abandon their religion. He also imposed other restrictions that made their lives very difficult. Soon the people of Jerusalem and Judea rose up in rebellion. This rebellion, led by Judah Maccabee and his brothers, lasted for three decades and was ultimately successful. For the first time since the Babylonian destruction more than 400 years before, Judea was free and sovereign.

The youngest of Judah Maccabee's brothers was Simon the Hasmonean. He and his sons and their descendents ruled the city for more than 80 years. These were, for the most part, years of growth and prosperity, although the royal household was constantly in turmoil. The city of Jerusalem became wealthy again, nearly 1,000 years after Solomon.

Herod

Confusion and civil strife in Rome made possible the rise to power of one of the most remarkable kings the world has ever known: Herod the Great. In 40 B.C. he was appointed—in Rome—king of Judea, though he did not take the throne until 37 B.C. Son of the prime minister of the kingdom, he was a friend of Mark Antony and later of Augustus Caesar. Herod was a brilliant and ruthless administrator, a spectacular builder, and an unhappy man. His wives (nine of them) and children (15), mothers-in-law, sons- and daughters-in-law, and his own mother and brothers seemed forever to be plotting against him. At least he thought they were, and many of them lost their lives because of it.

These problems did not affect Herod's building campaign, however. He ruled Jerusalem from 37 to 4 B.C., and there has never been a builder like him in the history of the city, possibly not in the whole world. What is now the Western ("Wailing") Wall in the Old City of Jerusalem was the gigantic retaining wall that Herod built to hold up the platform around his massive building of the Temple. Some of the stones weigh 70 to 80 tons. And the largest of the stones in the Wall is one of the largest stones ever cut—45 feet long, weighing more than 430 tons! (The largest stone in the Pyramids weighs only 15 tons). Herod's monumental building can be seen all over Jerusalem and throughout the land of Israel.

Jesus washes the feet of his disciples at the Last Supper.

Roman Jerusalem

When Herod died, the Romans were content to rule the country through his sons. When the sons died, or were deposed, a military governor was installed. These governors were called *procurators*. Pontius Pilate was the procurator who tried and condemned Jesus about A.D. 33. The city was at peace during those years, but the people resented the heavy hand of Rome. They were restless and unhappy. In such a volatile atmosphere, the teachings of Jesus of Nazareth found willing ears.

The Jews suffered under Roman rule. In the year A.D. 66, long-smoldering resentment broke out into open revolt. Nero, Emperor of Rome, sent three Roman Legions (5,000 soldiers each) to crush the revolt. After four years of fighting, the Legions destroyed Jerusalem and burnt the Temple. This happened in the late summer of the year A.D. 70, about 650 years after Nebuchadnezzar, king of Babylon, had destroyed the city for the first time.

The Romans still ruled over the city and the province of Judea. There were enough Jews left after the destruction to rebuild most of the town (but not the Temple). They continued to suffer under a harsh Roman government, until they rose again in revolt. The year was A.D. 130 and Hadrian was emperor of Rome. The second revolt lasted more than three years before it was crushed. This time the Romans were determined to put an end to the revolts. At the end of the war, Jerusalem was absolutely destroyed: "they plowed it with oxen and sprinkled it with salt" is the way a Jewish source describes what happened.

Hadrian rebuilt the city as a Roman pagan town. He forbade the Jews to live there, and changed its name to Aelia Capitolina. "Aelius" was the emperor's middle name. "Capitolina" was a reference to the god Jupiter, whose temple Hadrian built where the Jewish temple had once stood. Very little is known of the history of the city during this period. Today, part of the main Roman street ("the Cardo"), and the lower courses of Damascus Gate still exist. At one of the highest places in town, a Triumphal Arch can still be found in the Old City. These are the remains of Roman Jerusalem.

Golden coins from the second revolt, A.D. 130-133. The inscription reads, "To the freedom of Jerusalem."

The Via Dolorosa marks the path that Jesus walked on his way to Calvary.

Jerusalem of the Byzantines

Less than 200 years after Hadrian's rule, Emperor Constantine embraced Christianity and made it a lawful religion in the Roman empire (A.D. 313). He also moved his capital from Rome to the city of Byzantium, which he then renamed Constantinople (now called Istanbul).

For the second time, and to a second people, Jerusalem became the Holy City. As the scene of the last events in the life of Jesus, Jerusalem was filled with pilgrims and churches during these centuries. It was during this time that the name "Jerusalem" was restored.

Dozens of beautiful Byzantine churches were built for the Holy City between the fourth and seventh centuries. The most famous of them is the Church of the Holy Sepulchre. It marks the place where Jesus was crucified (Calvary) and buried (the tomb in the garden). Pilgrims have been coming to worship in this church every day for centuries. And the street that the Romans and Byzantines built down the center of the city (called "Cardo," from the Latin word for hinge) is still the main street of the Old City.

Arab Jerusalem

The Byzantine Era came to an end in the year 638. A new force conquered the Middle East and much of the rest of the world outside Europe. This force was Islam, and its soldiers were the Arabs.

The Arabs understood their new religion, Islam, as a continuation of the traditions of Judaism and Christianity, not as an independent creation. To Arabs, the pagans were contemptible, but the Jews and the Christians were "the people of the book." *Allah* is the same God as the Hebrew *Elohim*, Abraham is the father of both the Jews and the Muslims. The patriarchs and prophets—Noah, Lot, Moses, Aaron, Isaiah, Jeremiah, Jesus—are prophets for the Muslims as well. Thus, the Arabs were merciless in their treatment of the pagan populations of the countries they conquered (it was "Allah or the sword") but had to develop a special way of treating the Jews and Christians.

This was especially true in Jerusalem—which had now become the Holy City of a third group of people. The prophet Muhammed ordained that Muslim prayer be directed to Jerusalem. Thus the city became the original *Kiblah*, the direction Muslims face when praying. Only later was the direction of prayer changed to Mecca, the city (in modern day Saudi Arabia) where Islam began.

Arab historians report that the Byzantine king Sophronius was prepared to surrender Jerusalem only if the caliph himself, Umar ibn al-Khattab, came in person from Damascus to accept the surrender. Umar did indeed come to meet the king, the story continues, and had one principle request: He wished to see the site of the Temple of the Jews.

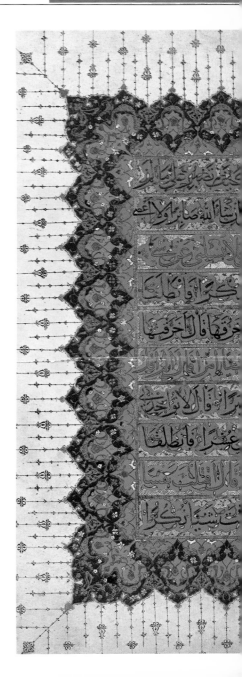

An elegant illuminated page from a sixteenth-century Koran, the holy book of Islam

When the king took him up on the Temple Mount—the same platform Herod had built 700 years earlier—the caliph was appalled at its condition. The Temple platform had become a garbage dump by then—intentionally made by the Byzantine Christians who wanted to show that Jesus' prophecy ("not one stone shall be left standing on another") had come to pass. Umar ordered the mount to be cleaned at once. The job of cleaning the platform was reported to have taken three full rainy seasons. But the Muslims, by taking over the Temple Mount, were making a very clear point: They were the legitimate successors to the revelation of the Jews.

Umar, the second caliph (634-644), is widely credited with determining the administration and law of the new Arab Empire. He is believed to be the author of the policy that fixed the rights (freedom from physical harm) and responsibilities (paying the poll tax) of the Jews and Christians in Jerusalem. While it is not certain that the law derived from Umar himself, the Muslim policy toward minorities was fairly consistent for the next 1,300 years, during which Jerusalem was an Arab city. The non-Muslim populations were left alone by the government. While they were not generally permitted to demonstrate their religion (processions and church bells were usually illegal in Jerusalem), Jews and Christians were not abused, provided they paid the poll tax and kept to themselves.

In 661, the caliphate was seized by the house of Umayya. This family was of old aristocratic background in Mecca. The Umayyad Dynasty ruled for less than 100 years, yet their contribution to Jerusalem was enormous. They began with a controversial political decision—to move the seat of the caliphate from Mecca to Damascus.

The old families of Mecca were furious at this move. They threatened to cut off Muslim pilgrimage to the holy Black Rock (the *Ka'ba*) in Mecca. Faced with the possibility of a full-scale rebellion in their empire, the Umayyad rulers decided to make Jerusalem so beautiful that it would substitute for Mecca as a focus of pilgrimage. To this end, they built palaces

The Dome of the Rock, atop the Temple Mount, is believed by Muslims to be the spot from which Muhammed ascended to heaven.

and mansions in the city. They also built a shrine where Herod's temple of the Jews and Hadrian's temple of the Romans had once stood.

The shrine is called the Dome of the Rock, so named because it covers the mountain peak above the City of David. This rock was traditionally the site of Moriah, where Abraham bound Isaac for sacrifice. It is also where Solomon built the Temple, around which Herod constructed the platform. For the Muslims, the rock was still the place of binding, except that the Koran retold the story of Abraham. The Koran said Abraham bound his other son, Ishmael, father of the Arabs. This was also the rock from which Muhammed ascended to heaven on his magical night journey to Jerusalem. The rock was holy, and it was thought that it might serve as an alternative to the Black Rock of Mecca. Eventually, the revolt was settled peacefully, the Dome of the Rock never did replace Mecca, but the shrine still stands. It was completed in 691, and it is one of the most beautiful buildings in the world.

The house of Umayya fell in the year 750, as a result of a revolt against them by their cousins, the Abbasids. This dynasty ruled until the middle of the thirteenth century. The early years of the Abbasid rule were the most glorious in Arab history, but none of that glory showed in Jerusalem. They neglected the city entirely, and there are almost no remains of the period to be seen today.

The Crusaders captured Jerusalem in 1099 and massacred its inhabitants.

The Crusades

Muslim Jerusalem lasted until the year 1099, when the city was conquered yet again, this time by the Crusaders—warriors, knights, priests, and peasants from every country in Europe. The Crusaders came to deliver the Holy Land from the hands of the Muslims. They surrounded Jerusalem, scaled the north

The Church of the Holy Sepulchre encloses Calvary and the tomb of Jesus.

wall (on July 15, 1099), and massacred the inhabitants. Thousands of people died that day: the Muslims were killed on the Temple Mount and the Jews were burned alive in their synagogues, until there was, at last, nobody left to kill. It seemed as if the city would never recover. But somehow, Jerusalem was able to rise again.

The Crusaders, though they held Jerusalem for fewer than 100 years, rebuilt the ruined city with astonishing speed and energy. The Citadel of Jerusalem, the heart of the Church of the Holy Sepulchre, and many more of the city's finest churches date from the years of their rule. The Crusaders converted the Dome of the Rock and mosques into churches and dwellings. Jews and Muslims were forbidden to live within the walls of the city, though the rule was relaxed slightly by the middle of the twelfth century. The Latin Kingdom of Jerusalem flourished for a while, but lack of political unity and increasing pressure from Islam proved to be too much for the Crusaders to withstand.

Saladin, the great Kurdish general, expelled the Crusaders in 1187. King Richard the Lion Heart of England tried to recapture the city five years later but was not successful. A smaller Crusader Kingdom was established until the Muslims finally took over for good in the 1250s. From then until 1917, Jerusalem remained under Arab control.

In 1250, the Mamelukes overthrew the Egyptians and became the rulers of Jerusalem.

Mamelukes and Turks

Saladin and his sons ruled the country for two generations. Then, for more than 250 years, Jerusalem was ruled by one of the strangest political groups the world has ever known. They were called Mamelukes, and they were tribesmen from the steppes of central Asia. Taken as slaves into Egypt, they were freed from slavery at age 18 to become a permanent class of soldiers. In 1250, this warrior class overthrew the government of Egypt and inherited its provinces (Jerusalem was one). They ruled like military dictators. Each ruler held on to power until he died, was unseated, assassinated, or otherwise replaced by one of his fellows.

The Mamelukes were a violent and lawless group, but one of the rules of their system had a profound influence on Jerusalem, Damascus, and Cairo—their three great cities. This was the rule that a Mameluke could not leave either his kingdom or his wealth to his sons. They were therefore obliged to spend their money, and this resulted in a building campaign of remarkable proportions. They built mansions, court-houses, tombs, and especially religious seminaries (*madrasahs*) throughout the city. Many of Jerusalem's most beautiful and unique buildings are of Mameluke origin.

Jerusalem was a Mameluke city until 1517. That year the city fell into the hands of the greatest of all the Muslim empires, the Ottoman Turks. They established a capital in Constantinople, which they renamed Istanbul. Their new capital was in Asia Minor, renamed Turkey.

The Turkish sultan Suleiman was called "the Magnificent," for he ruled over an empire of unimaginable luxury and splendor. He encouraged both Christians and Jews to settle in his empire, and the years of his long rule (1520-1566) are remembered as years of peace and prosperity. The work of Sultan Suleiman can be seen every day in Jerusalem. It was he who built the walls that now stand around the Old City, finishing the work in the year 1538.

The Ottoman Empire ruled Jerusalem for 400 years, but its glory did not survive the passing of

Suleiman the Magnificent. The empire broke up into petty states ruled by corrupt governors, princes, rebels, and bandits. Often, the land and the city lapsed into lawlessness and anarchy, with only small attention being paid to the sultan in Istanbul. This is one of the few periods in the history of Jerusalem whose remains cannot be seen today (apart from the walls around the city). Nothing happened during this time; the city simply fell apart. Travelers who saw it in the eighteenth and nineteenth centuries all described the same scene: poverty, misery, dirt, and disease.

A sixteenth-century woodcut shows Jerusalem as it appeared looking west from the Mount of Olives.

Toward the end of this period after Suleiman, in the 1860s, people started to leave the terrible conditions of the Old City. They moved their houses and neighborhoods outside the city walls. From this point, the history of modern Jerusalem begins.

Modern Jerusalem

By the middle of the nineteenth century, European colonial powers—Britain, France, Germany, and Russia—had begun to be interested in the Holy City. At first their interest was charitable and religious. European churches, hospitals, and neighborhoods were built both inside and outside the walls of the Old City. But very soon the matter was political as well. The Holy Land quickly became an object of colonialism.

Turkey joined the German side of World War I. By 1918, the war was over, Germany was defeated, and the Ottoman Empire had collapsed. The victorious allies, Britain and France, divided the empire. The League of Nations awarded France a mandate to govern Syria; Britain, which had fought bloody battles in the region, received a mandate over the area they called by its old Roman, Byzantine, and European name: Palestine.

Jerusalem was now well governed for the first time in almost 400 years. The city was largely cleaned up and rebuilt during the days of the Mandate. Many large new neighborhoods—Jewish, Christian, and

The Rockefeller Museum, built during the British Mandate, houses archeological displays and is located in east Jerusalem.

General Allenby (right) and British governor of Jerusalem, Ronald Storrs (left), tour the city in 1920.

Muslim—grew up outside the walls of the Old City during those years. Some of the city's most famous modern landmarks—The Rockefeller Museum, Government House, and the YMCA—date from the period of the Mandate.

After World War II, the British understood that they could no longer govern the country. Pressure came from the Jewish people, who had just endured the horrors of the Nazi Holocaust in Europe. Other pressure came from the Arabs, who had been promised many things by the British (through Lawrence of Arabia) in return for their support in World War I. All these pressures created a situation of unbearable tension.

The YMCA building is a fine example of architecture from the British Mandate days.

The Jews demanded that the remnants of their people be gathered back in the land of Israel. The Arabs feared that their centuries-old control over Jerusalem was slipping out of their grasp. The majority of the population of Jerusalem (then more than 165,000) was already Jewish, and had been since the 1850s.

The British were plagued with massive problems in India and weakened to the point of exhaustion by the damage the war had done to their own country. They could not also maintain control of Palestine, so the British simply gave up. In the spring of 1947, they announced their intention to return the mandate they had been given for Palestine. The problem was now international, in the care of the newly formed United Nations.

After a series of meetings with all parties to the dispute, the United Nations Special Committee on Palestine (UNSCOP) submitted its recommendations to the Secretary General. The recommendation was for the partition of Palestine into a Jewish State and an Arab State. Jerusalem was awarded special international status as an international regime, to be administered by the United Nations. Interestingly, the boundaries of this special city were almost identical to those of Hadrian's Aelia Capitolina 1,800 years before. On November 29, 1947, the General Assembly voted to accept the Special Committee's recommendations.

During World War II, millions of Jews were forced into concentration camps where they were tortured and murdered by the Nazis. This period is now referred to as the Holocaust.

The War of 1948

The Jewish authorities accepted the partition plan, although unhappily. They knew the loss of Jerusalem meant the loss of one-sixth of the Jewish population in the Jewish State (which was then 650,000). And the emotional shock of being cut off from the ancient capital was enormous. But the partition plan was never implemented. The Arabs, both those living in the country and those in nations around Israel, rejected the partition plan. The Arabs declared war on the Jewish State.

The attacks began the next day, and within a week the country plunged into war. Between December 1947 and May 1948 Jerusalem suffered siege and bloodshed as the two sides battled. On May 14, 1948, the British left Palestine. The next day, the State of Israel was declared. At this point, the war

When Israel achieved independence, in 1948, it was at war with all of its Arab neighbors.

widened in scope and intensity. Israel was invaded by the armies of Egypt, Lebanon, Syria, Iraq, and Transjordan at the same time. The war of 1948 continued throughout the year and into January, 1949. But the fate of Jerusalem had long since been decided.

A Divided City

By May 1948, the Old City and the neighborhoods immediately to the east, north, and south of it were firmly in the hands of the Jordanians, who had fought to save the local population. The defenders of the Jewish quarter of the Old City had surrendered on May 27th. Thirteen hundred women, children, and old men were settled in the western part of the city. Others were sent to captivity in Transjordan. The Jordanians destroyed nearly every synagogue and large Jewish institutional building in the Old City. The Jewish quarter was largely reduced to rubble.

West Jerusalem was in the hands of the Israelis. Thus, the city sat divided between 1948 and 1967. Minefields, concrete walls, and rings of barbed wire separated the Jewish half of the city from the Old City and the Arab areas.

Israel declared Jerusalem to be its capital in 1949 and moved the rest of its national institutions to the city. This decision remains a subject of dispute. Many foreign governments argued that the 1947 United Nations partition plan is the last legal document concerning the city. They argued that the rest was the result of war. They believed no major decision about the city could be made without a peace treaty between Israel and its Arab neighbors.

In 1951, Transjordan annexed areas west of the Jordan River (called the West Bank) and changed the name of the kingdom to the Hashemite Kingdom of Jordan. The annexation included the Old City of Jerusalem and the Arab areas around it. The Jordanian annexation of Jerusalem was not recognized by any country in the world except Pakistan.

The western (Jewish) part of the city doubled in population after 1948. National institutions were built during those years: the Knesset (parliament), the Hebrew University campus at Givat Ram, the Israel Museum, Hadassah Hospital, Yad Va-Shem Holocaust Memorial, and others.

There was less development in the Old City and East Jerusalem, as the Jordanians devoted most of

The Knesset, or parliament building, was built soon after independence.

their efforts to building up the east bank. The population of East Jerusalem (65,000 people) remained constant during those years, with an interesting demographic change: The Muslim population grew from about 40,000 to 55,000 while the Christian population shrank from 25,000 to 10,000.

The Six-Day War of 1967

In 1967, war erupted again. Israel had come into conflict with Egypt over the Suez Canal and the Sinai Peninsula. Messages were passed through the United Nations to King Hussein of Jordan, advising him not to become involved in a war that was not in any way directed against him. But by the morning of June 5th, 1967, Jerusalem was under artillery barrage from the Jordanians. A column of Jordanian infantry had launched an attack on the Government House complex, and Jerusalem found itself at war again.

This time the battle was over in two days, and Israel gained possession of the entire area that had been British Mandate Palestine. Jerusalem was, at last, reunited. And the Muslim and Christian inhabitants of East Jerusalem found themselves yet again under the rule of foreigners. They had been ruled by Romans, Persians, Byzantines, by Arabs from Damascus and Baghdad, by Crusaders from Europe, Mamelukes, Turks, British, and Jordanians. Now they were ruled by the Israelis.

Israeli bulldozers had to clear away the rubble of the 1967 War from the area around the Wailing Wall to provide space for religious services.

In June, 1967, victorious Israeli troops passed freely through the Mandelbaum gate, which once separated Jordanian and Israeli Jerusalem.

Today, the Old City has been cleaned, repaved, and rebuilt. The Jewish quarter inside the Old City walls, destroyed by the war of 1948 and subsequent neglect, has been reconstructed. In digging the foundations for new buildings, archaeologists have discovered spectacular remains of past glory: the grand Umayyad palaces of the seventh century; Justinian's New Church of St. Mary, the Nea (sixth century); the Broad Wall of Hezekiah (eighth century B.C.), and 25,000 square feet of mansion buildings from the Herodian Quarter of Jerusalem (first century B.C.-A.D.).

Outside the walls, new houses, neighborhoods, hotels, and office buildings have risen. The old Mount Scopus campus of the Hebrew University has been built anew and a plain downtown shopping street has been converted into a busy and colorful

Modern buildings co-exist with ancient ones throughout Jerusalem. By law all new buildings must be constructed from the same native limestone that gives the city its golden glow.

pedestrian mall. A stretch of wilderness at the edge of the desert far to the south of town has become a promenade that will one day reach all the way to the Old City. Flowers bloom in a hundred corners of a hundred streets. Jerusalem is clean, beautiful, well governed, and well kept, but the people have not yet learned to live in peace with each other.

By the 1970s and early 1980s, the Arabs of East Jerusalem had more or less come to terms with Israeli rule. For the most part, they declined the offer of citizenship by the Israeli government. Yet many voted in periodic municipal elections (it was impossible, however, to find an Arab candidate for the still-vacant post of Deputy Mayor). Without dealing with the basic political problems affecting the area, a "way of life" was established to enable the city to function. And it did indeed function. Jerusalem did not redivide. Nor did it become Belfast or Beirut, cities in which large-scale murder and destruction became the order of the day.

The basic political problems were not, however, suppressed forever. In December 1987, riots in Gaza spread to the West Bank and to Arab Jerusalem, and all the old resentments resurfaced. The *intifada* (Arab uprising) continued through 1988 and 1989, and only at the beginning of 1990 were there signs that the uprising had lost momentum. Merchants had been forced to close their shops every day at noon in protest of the Israeli occupation. When a general strike was called, the merchants of East Jerusalem and the Old City were forced to close for the entire day. These protests caused the merchants great economic damage. The uprisings also affected Israel's tourism industry and its political support overseas. With the start of the Persian Gulf War on January 17, 1991, Israel's security was once again greatly threatened. Saddam Hussein of Iraq had pledged that Israel would be his first target in the event of a war. He proved true to his word. On the morning of the second day of the war, Iraq fired eight Scud missiles at Israel. Some of the missiles missed their targets, but a few landed in Tel Aviv. Others had come dangerously close to Jerusalem. More bombings would follow in the coming weeks. The attacks against Israel immediately brought the country into a war it wanted to avoid. Palestinians were overjoyed by the attacks, and Iraq's aggression gave these Arabs new hope that Israel would soon crumble. Arab uprisings began to crop up throughout the occupied West Bank. Some primitive missile-rockets were even fired by Palestinians, but these attacks were quickly stopped by the Israeli military.

Once again, Israel had come under siege. As weeks went by, citizens of Jerusalem and Tel Aviv spent night after night huddled together in sealed rooms, wearing gas masks. And each day that the war raged on took the Arabs and Jews one step further away from ever living together in peace.

The *intifada,* or uprising, brought many Palestinians into the streets to demonstrate for their independence.

THE PEOPLE

I give you the end of a golden string;
Only wind it into a ball, It will lead you in
at Heaven's gate, Built in Jerusalem's wall.
                                    —William Blake

The Mahaneh Yehuda fruit and vegetable market offers a
wealth of fresh produce.

The mayor of Jerusalem, Teddy Kollek, is popular with most of the residents of the city.

A century ago, Jerusalem was a city of 25,000 people. It has grown 20-fold since then, and most of the growth is due to the influx of populations from elsewhere. The result is a mix that surprises visitors. In a city of fewer than half a million inhabitants, there are 140 distinct ethnic communities and 100 different languages!

To be sure, every large city has people of different types and races. But Jerusalem is, first of all, not very large. And it is different from most cities in that many of its people often wear their traditional costumes. There is great variety in the character of different neighborhoods, and equally great variety in the look of the people who inhabit them.

Some neighborhoods are modern and nonreligious. In those places one sees Jews or Arabs in business suits, jeans, slacks, skirts, and dresses—just like anywhere else. Yet even in supposedly nonreligious neighborhoods one always finds men and women—usually older—who still wear a traditional non-Western dress. This is especially true among the Arabs, and among Jews who came from places like India, Kurdistan, Morocco, Syria, Iraq, Russian Georgia, Bukhara, and Yemen.

Other neighborhoods are religious. In Jewish areas, one sees that most of the women cover their hair and wear long dresses. The men always wear hats or skull-caps. In Arab areas, one finds religious Muslim women wearing a long coat-dress that covers

The *kefiyeh* is the traditional Arab headwear.

The mosque at the foot of the Mount of Olives

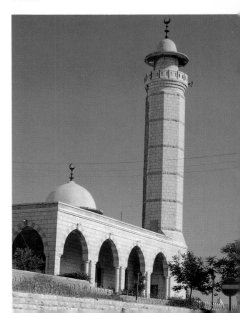

their entire body, from neck to ankles and wrists. Their head, except for the face, is completely covered with a white scarf. Arab men often wear a white or checkered scarf, the *kefiyeh,* with a double ring of black rope holding it down.

Still other neighborhoods in Jewish Jerusalem are ultra-orthodox. Here one sees men with full beards and side curls, young men and even small boys all wearing long black coats and wide-brim hats. Ultra-orthodox Jewish women shave their heads and wear either a wig or only a scarf.

Clergymen are everywhere in Jerusalem: Greek and Russian Orthodox, Roman Catholic, Armenian, Coptic, Ethiopian, and Assyrian priests. Each in his traditional dress and unique style hat. There are monks and nuns of many orders of the Catholic church, all in their distinctive dress.

All over town one finds Bedouin nomads who have come in from the outlying desert. It is not easy to distinguish the Bedouin men from other Arabs, but Bedouin women are instantly recognizable by their colorful dress, embroidered by hand in traditional patterns. Many have tattooed faces. They often come into the city to sell vegetables, spices, or fruits they have grown. It is not uncommon to see half a dozen Bedouin women sitting on the sidewalk selling vegetables from a basket outside a modern super-market.

In areas where many different kinds of people meet—the markets, downtown shopping areas, and the Old City—Jerusalem mixes thousands of tourists and pilgrims. These people include Americans, Europeans, Chinese, Korean, Japanese, Greeks, Cypriots, Africans, and South Americans. The combination of people and costumes one sees in Jerusalem is quite beyond what one would expect from a city of its size. It is like being in New York, Paris, Moscow, Cairo, Crakow, Bombay, Baghdad, Casablanca, Tiblisi, and Sa'ana—all at the same time!

Bedouin women often enter the city from the desert to sell vegetables or spices they have grown.

The Me'a Sha'arim quarter is home to many ultra-orthodox Jews.

ON THE TOUR BUS

A visit to Jerusalem always starts with the Old City, which is a smaller area than one would expect from so much history. You can walk from any side of the Old City to the opposite side in 15 minutes. It is the sheer volume of sites and history that compels the visitor to take plenty of time for seeing the Old City.

The Old City
Museums

The Tower of David Museum of the History of Jerusalem, inside the citadel at Jaffa Gate. This massive Crusader fortress building, with archaeology dating back to the days of King Herod, houses an audiovisual presentation of 4,000 years of Jerusalem's history. Models, pictures, films and reconstructions, plus spectacular views of the city from the walls and towers. There is a sound and light show on summer nights.

The Armenian Art Museum. Located in a beautiful building in the Armenian quarter, the museum contains pictures and

text about the history of the Armenians.

The Islamic Museum. A medieval vaulted building on the Temple Mount containing objects of Muslim history and religion from Jerusalem, especially handwritten books and scrolls.

Near the Jaffa Gate

Archaeological and Historical Sites

The excavations of the City of David, at the City of David, below the Dung Gate. A massive terraced structure of the Solomonic city and many buildings of the Canaanite city before Solomon and the Biblical city after Solomon. Public works of Biblical Jerusalem include a tunnel access to the water supply of Gihon spring ("Warren's shaft") and a 1,700-foot tunnel cut into bedrock ("Hezekiah's tunnel") to bring spring water from outside the walls to the Siloam pool inside the walls.

The Broad Wall and Israelite Tower, in the Jewish quarter. A massive wall and towers of the eighth and seventh centuries B.C.

The First Wall. Built by Simon the Hasmonean in the second century B.C., pieces of this wall are to be seen under the present city walls south of Jaffa Gate and along the Cardo in the Jewish quarter.

The Herodian Quarter, in the Jewish quarter. The lower floors of 6 mansions with a total of 25,000 square feet. These luxurious buildings, dating from Jerusalem in the days of Jesus, feature period furniture, mosaics, pottery, frescos, stonework, and glass.

The Burnt House, in the Jewish quarter. Ashes cover the ruins of this Jerusalem house destroyed by the Roman legions in A.D. 70.

The Western (Wailing) Wall excavations, near the Dung Gate. Umayyid palaces have been cut through to reveal massive Herodian building arches, streets, and shops outside the Temple Mount. Stones of 70-80 tons are set into the Wall. On the south wall are a monumental stairway and the remains of gates. Byzantine houses built over the site can be seen, and marble columns are scattered about.

Prayers left in the Wailing Wall

Damascus Gate. The oldest gate in the city, from Aelia Capitolina of Hadrian in the second century A.D. Here are the original staircases and paving, with pictures, models, and maps depicting Damascus Gate through the ages. It may be reached by walking on top of the city walls from Jaffa Gate (an exciting walk).

The Cardo, in the Jewish quarter. Reconstruction of the main street of Byzantine Jerusalem from the fifth to seventh centuries A.D. Adjoining reconstruction of Crusader markets along the same street.

The Hurva Synagogue, in the Jewish quarter. Remains of the largest synagogue in Jerusalem, finished mid-nineteenth century, and dynamited by the Arab

Legion after the fall of the Jewish quarter in May 1948.

Jewish Holy Places

The Western Wall. Called "the Wailing Wall" by Christians and Muslims (but not by Jews), the Wall became holy to the Jews after Turkish times. Eleven layers of monumental stones support Herod's platform around the Temple. There is a constant presence of men and women at prayer.

David's Tomb, on Mount Zion. Used as synagogue, church, and mosque from about the second century A.D. to the present. A crusader marker is over the supposed site of David's tomb. Interesting old architecture.

Christian Holy Places

The Via Dolorosa, in the Muslim quarter. A street leading from the site of the Antonia

Along the Cardo

Along the Via Dolorosa

fortress to the church of the Holy Sepulchre, revered as the route Jesus supposedly took on his way to crucifixion. An interesting walk through markets and stores of the Old City, with 14 "Stations of the Cross"—chapels and churches—along the way marking events in the last day of Jesus. Stations 9 through 14 are inside the Church of the Holy Sepulchre. There are organized pilgrimages by the Franciscans every Friday afternoon.

The Church of the Holy Sepulchre, in the Christian Quarter. The church encloses Calvary and the Tomb of Jesus. The rotunda and church were begun by Constantine the Great in the fourth century; A Crusader church filled the interior spaces. Armenian excavations below reveal a seventh century B.C. stone quarry.

The Ecce Homo, between second and third stations of the Cross. Hadrian's Triumphal Arch incorporated into a nineteenth century church. In the basement are extensive remains of floors and storage pools of Herod's Antonia fortress.

The Cenacle, on Mount Zion. The traditional site of the Upper Room, in which the Last Supper was held. Crusader architecture.

The Church of the Holy Sepulchre

The Church of St. Anne, in the Muslim quarter near the Lions Gate. Traditional site of the birth of the Virgin Mary, next to the pools of Bethesda. There are interesting walks through the antiquities of the pool. The inside of the old Crusader church has amazing acoustics.

Muslim Holy Places
The Haram esh Sharif ("The Noble Sanctuary"), on the Temple Mount. Here are the Dome of the Rock, Al Aqsa Mosque, an Islamic museum, and innumerable small shrines.

Exquisite spaces and buildings. Access to some of the sites is limited.

Outside the Walls
Museums
The Israel Museum. Archaeology, painting, sculpture, ethnography, Judaica, and the Dead Sea Scrolls pavilion, brilliantly designed and presented, make this one of the finest museums in the world.

Yad va-Shem Holocaust Memorial, Mount Herzl. A museum, art exhibition, sculpture, memorial chapels, and monuments devoted to the destruction of European Jewry by the Nazis and their allies.

The Rockefeller Museum, in East Jerusalem, opposite the Flower gate, near the northeast corner of the Old City. An old-fashioned display of archaeology in a beautiful Mandate building.

The Museum of Islamic Art, Palmah Street. An exquisite collection of Muslim art; museum of clocks and watches in basement.

The Turgeman Post, near the Mandelbaum gate. The museum, housed in a former army position, depicts the divided city of Jerusalem, 1948-1967.

Landmarks

The Mount of Olives. The most spectacular view of the Old City, from the lookout at the top of the mountain. The chapel of the Ascension and the grotto of the Lord's Prayer are at the top.

A walk down to the Kidron passes the Jewish cemetery (70,000 graves), tombs attributed to the prophets, the church of Dominus Flevit (The Lord Wept over Jerusalem), and the Russian and Franciscan churches of the Garden of Gethsemane.

The Model of Second Temple Jerusalem, at the Holyland Hotel in Bayit ve-Gan. A reconstruction (on a scale of 1:50) of Jerusalem in the year A.D. 66, the year of the outbreak of the revolt against Rome, when the city was at its largest and most magnificent. Invaluable for understanding major architectural features of the city: the walls, the Citadel, the Temple and its platform, the Antonia, the City of David, Mount Zion, etc. Sightseeing trips should begin here.

The Chagall windows at Hadassah, in Ein Karem. Twelve famous stained glass

panels decorate the synagogue of the Hadassah Hospital.

The Biblical Zoo, Romema. All the animals mentioned in the Bible.

The Lookout Plazas at Mount Scopus, near the Hebrew University campus on Mount Scopus. One famous view over the Old City to the west, and another (further south) over the Judean desert to the east. Both views are very impressive.

The Promenade, near Government House complex in East Talpiyot. Newly constructed promenade with marvelous views toward the desert in one direction and the city of Jerusalem in the other. Best place to see the exact location of the City of David.

The Kidron Valley, below the City of David and Silwan Village. Monumental carved Jewish tombs from the first century B.C. to the first century A.D.

Ein Karem. A very picturesque old village, famous as the birthplace of John the Baptist, and now a Jewish neighborhood on the western edge of Jerusalem. Not extensively built since its abandonment in 1948 but restored to original style. It has the most authentic Arabic village architecture in the country and many churches.

The Israel Museum houses the Dead Sea Scrolls.

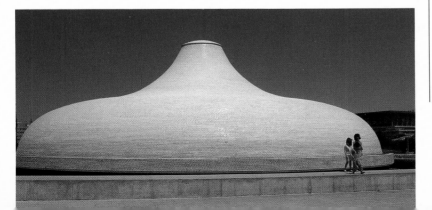

CHRONOLOGY

B.C.

2000	First recorded mention of Jerusalem.
1000	David becomes king of united kingdom of Judah and Israel, with Jerusalem as capital; returns Ark of Covenant to city.
c. 965–928	Reign of King Solomon; building of first Temple.
721	Assyrians destroy Israel; Jerusalem spared.
586	Destruction of city by Babylonians.
c. 520	Small group of Jews returns from exile to rebuild city walls and Temple.
332	Conquest by Alexander the Great.
165	Revolt led by Judah Maccabee.
63	Jerusalem captured by Roman general Pompey
37–4	Reign of King Herod the Great.

A.D.

33	Trial and execution of Jesus of Nazareth.
66	Outbreak of the great revolt against Rome.
70	Roman Legions crush revolt, destroying the city and burning the Temple.
130	Second revolt against Roman rule.
135	End of revolt; building of Aelia Capitolina.
323	Emperor Constantine moves capital from Rome to Byzantium.
638	Muslim conquest of city.
691	Completion of Dome of the Rock.
1099	Crusader conquest.
1187	Saladin expels Crusaders from city.
1250	Capture of city by Mamelukes.
1517	Capture of city by Ottoman Turks.
1917	Capture of the city by the British.
1920	Beginning of British Mandate.
1947	United Nations votes to partition Palestine into a Jewish state and an Arab state; Jerusalem given special status to be administered by U.N.
1948	City divided as a result of 1948 war.
1949	Israel declares Jerusalem its capital.
1967	Six Day War results in reunification of city.
1987	*Intifada* begins.
1991	Persian Gulf War begins.

For Further Reading

Aharoni, Yohanan, and Michael Avi-Yonah. *The Macmillan Bible Atlas.* Macmillan, 1977.
Churchill, Randolph and Winston. *The Six-Day War.* Heinemann, 1967.
Collins, Larry, and Dominique Lapierre. *O Jerusalem!* Pocket Book, 1973.
Connolly, Peter. *Living in the Time of Jesus of Nazareth.* Oxford, 1983.
Gilbert, Martin. *The Arab-Israel Conflict, Its History in Maps.* Weidenfeld & Nicholson, 1984.
Gur, Mordechai. *The Battle for Jerusalem.* Popular Library, 1974.
Hoade, Eugene. *Guide to the Holy Land.* 7th ed. Franciscan Press (Jerusalem), 1973.
Kollek, Teddy, and Moshe Pearlman. *Jerusalem, Sacred City of Mankind,* rev. ed. Weidenfeld & Nicholson, 1974.
Peters, F. E. *Jerusalem.* Princeton University, 1985.
Phillips, John. *The Will to Survive.* Dial Press, 1977.
Prittie, Terence. *Whose Jerusalem?* Frederick Muller, 1981.
Vilnay, Zev. *Legends of Jerusalem.* Jewish Publication Society, 1973.

Where to Get More Information

Further information about Jerusalem may be found at any branch of the *Israel Government Tourist Office:*

NEW YORK
350 Fifth Avenue
19th Floor
New York, NY 10018
Tel. (212) 560-0650

CHICAGO
5 South Wabash Avenue
Chicago, IL 60603
Tel. (312) 782-4306

DALLAS
Suite 1810
Dallas, TX 75251
Tel. (214) 991-9097

LOS ANGELES
6180 Wilshire Boulevard
Los Angeles, CA 90048
Tel. (213) 658-7462

MIAMI
25 SE Second Avenue
Suite 745
Miami, FL 33131
(305) 539-1919

INDEX

Photo credits
Cover, page 33, Steve Vidler/Leo de Wys Inc.; p. 4–5, 13, 14, 15, 16, 18–19, 20, 21, 36, 40, 42, 45, 48, 50–51, 53 (bottom), 55, 56, 57, (bottom-left, top), 58, 59, Dalia Migdal; p. 8–9, Dani Waxman; p. 21, 29, Israel Museum; p. 25, The British Museum; p. 30, American Colony, Jerusalem; p. 31, The Bettmann Archive; p. 35, Illustration by Gustave Doré; p. 37, Yoram Lehmann/The Tower of David Museum of the History of Jerusalem; p. 41, Beth Hatefutsoth Photo Archive; p. 43, Yad va-Shem Museum; p. 44, 46, 47, UPI/Bettmann Newsphotos; p. 49, 57 (bottom-right), Reuters/Bettmann; p. 52, Jacky/The Office of the Mayor, Jerusalem; p. 53 (bottom), Karen McCunnal/Leo de Wys Inc.; p. 54, Mike Busselle/Leo de Wys Inc.